Original title:

In the Shadow of Paradise

Copyright © 2025 Creative Arts Management OÜ
All rights reserved.

Author: Elias Marchant
ISBN HARDBACK: 978-1-80581-659-1
ISBN PAPERBACK: 978-1-80581-186-2
ISBN EBOOK: 978-1-80581-659-1

Beneath the Arc of Blissful Illusions

Under hopes that float like bubbles,
We dance in circles, dodging troubles.
A jester's hat, all bright and bold,
Worn by dreams that never get old.

The cake is slice, yet crumbs appear,
We munch on laughter, never fear.
With pie in hand, we paint the skies,
While sneaky cats plot their surprise.

Veils of Enchantment and Despair

A magic show where ducks can fly,
With capes of cloth, we wave goodbye.
Yet whispers crawled from corners deep,
They tickle fancies, then make us weep.

Balancing on stilts made of joy,
Stepping lightly, like a toy.
When mirrors crack, we just grin wide,
For every fall, there's still a ride.

The Solitude of Sugarcoated Realities

Candy-coated dreams on a sunny morn,
With gumdrop fancies ready to be worn.
Yet lurking 'neath the icing's glaze,
Are pickled fears and avocado craze.

We twirl around, our shirts untucked,
Life's a joke that's inexplicably plucked.
In lollipop fields, we laugh and wrestle,
With sprinkles stuck in hair, a true vessel.

Chasing Fading Zinnias

In gardens where the sunflowers tease,
We trip on roots, bring bees to sneeze.
Oh, how the zinnias joyfully fade,
While we misplace our jokes in the shade.

As butterflies waltz, we mimic their style,
With goofy grins, we stay awhile.
And though colors wilt and moments twist,
We laugh at the chaos, it's hard to resist.

Reflections in a Crystal Pool

I gazed into the water's sheen,
My reflection looked quite serene.
Yet bubbles rose with every sigh,
Did my hair just wave goodbye?

A frog jumped in with a splash and croak,
It winked at me like it was a joke.
"You think you're grand, with your fancy looks?"
Said the frog while reading my story books.

The fish just laughed, they swam on by,
Chasing their tails and the dragonfly.
In this pool where all seems fine,
I ponder if the frog likes wine.

Sunlight danced on the silver spray,
Making shadows in a cheerful way.
But I must confess, it's hard to think,
When all I want is a drink and wink.

Whispers of a Forgotten Realm

I wandered through a field of dreams,
Where nothing's ever what it seems.
A hedgehog offered me a snack,
I declined, it looked like a backpack.

The trees were gossiping quite loud,
About the antics of a cloud.
"Did you see how it flipped and fell?"
Butterflies laughed, their wings did swell.

Around a corner, what did I find?
A cactus dressed in purple, blind!
It swayed to music no one heard,
While twirling like a frisky bird.

In this realm where oddities play,
Laughter echoes night and day.
Perhaps I'll stay just one more hour,
To dance with cacti, full of power.

The Charm of Elusive Dreams

I chased a dream that slipped away,
Like jellybeans on a sunny day.
It giggled loud as I fell flat,
And transformed into a dancing cat.

The moon peeked out, grinning wide,
While I stumbled on this joyful ride.
"Hey there, friend, come join the fun!"
Said a star who sparkled like the sun.

Together we twirled in twilight's hue,
With dreamy folks in pointy shoes.
A parade of oddities down the lane,
Where even a spoon could hold a reign!

But then I woke and found no prize,
Just an empty cup and sleepy eyes.
Yet in my heart, that dance remained,
And laughter echoed, unchained.

Under the Blooming Cloud of Memory

Under clouds that bloom and sway,
I found my thoughts just hideaway.
They popped like popcorn in a breeze,
All sprawled out, doing as they please.

A memory dressed in polka dots,
Said, "Don't you dare forget the knots!"
It tied my shoes and skipped away,
Leaving me in quite a dismay.

A squirrel brought nuts in a bag,
And sang a song, oh what a rag!
It slipped on leaves that just said, "Hi!"
And danced beneath the autumn sky.

So here I sit, with blooms galore,
Tickled by thoughts, I can't ignore.
Under laughter and memories bright,
I twirl and spin in pure delight.

Shades of Serenity in the Abyss

In a land where giggles thrive,
The gloom and grumble take a dive.
Silly hats and playful jests,
Even shadows wear their vests.

A panda stole my lunch today,
Then pranced around in bright ballet.
Laughter echoes through the trees,
While squirrels join in to tease.

The sun pretends to take a nap,
While mice in suits begin to clap.
They juggle moonbeams, one, two, three,
And serve up pies with glee and spree.

So in this space of strange delight,
Where chuckles dance with pure delight,
Remember, joy can surely bloom,
Even when hiding in the gloom.

The Dance of Twilit Shadows

Two ducks waddle in a line,
Holding hands, they sip on brine.
Their tap dance stirs the twilight dew,
Announcing fun with every shoe.

A cat in shades plays the guitar,
Singing songs from near and far.
The stars groan in a twinkling spree,
As rabbits bop in jubilee.

In corners bright, the shadows sip,
On lemonade and friendship's trip.
Laughter bubbles, snickers fly,
As night drops down from azure sky.

Oh, join the merry, happy throng,
Where everything feels right and wrong.
For even shadows need a chance,
To join in on the weirdest dance.

The Palette of Untapped Joy

Brush strokes of laughter paint the air,
With hues of mischief everywhere.
Candied clouds float on a whim,
While rainbows wear their shiny trim.

A fox wearing glasses reads a book,
While squirrels in bowties come to look.
They plot to mix a fizzy brew,
With popcorn, jelly, and glue too!

Tickles hide in places snug,
While giggles cozy like a bug.
The moon goes green, the stars turn pink,
In this bizarre space where we think.

So grab your brushes, paint the night,
With swirls of giggles, oh what a sight!
For joy is a palette, wild and bright,
Just waiting for your heart's delight.

Whispers Beneath the Weeping Willows

Beneath the willows, jokes unfold,
A wise old owl tells tales retold.
With branches swaying, laughter stirs,
As frogs recite their silly purrs.

The wind's a trickster, plays around,
Stealing hats and dancing sound.
While fireflies twinkle, full of cheer,
They whisper secrets that we hold dear.

A raccoon wearing a shiny ring,
Plays the accordion, what a fling!
The night is filled with chirps and charms,
As dreams gather in their cozy farms.

So linger here, let laughter flow,
For under the willows, the good vibes glow.
In every giggle and softly spun tale,
Life's little wonders will never fail.

Where Wishes Tangle with Reality

In a land where dreams collide,
A talking frog I tried to ride.
He croaked a tune, I laughed so loud,
He claimed to be the king, so proud.

With wishes woven in a ball,
I tossed them high, they did not fall.
A silly dance, a wobbly jig,
I flailed around like a giant pig.

Reality, a playful ghost,
Chasing me while I just boast.
With every twist of fate I see,
My wishes laugh right back at me.

A potion brewed with stars and sun,
Turns out it was a big, fat pun.
So here I am, a chuckling fool,
In a world where nothing follows rule.

Secrets We Bury in the Earth

In the garden, secrets lie,
Cabbages whisper while they sigh.
Potatoes hide with fear of spiders,
While carrots cling to earth like wipers.

I dug a hole for dreams so bright,
Only to find a shoe in fright.
An old sock grinned, 'Your choice was poor!'
I laughed, then slipped and tumbled more.

The artichokes stand tall, so wise,
While peas peek out with watchful eyes.
What's buried deep beneath the dirt,
Are hints of laughter, secrets flirt.

Old bones of humor, here to play,
Who knew they'd brighten up my day?
In the earth, where secrets cheer,
We plant our hopes, and forget our fear.

The Veil of Lamented Happiness

Beneath a veil, so fine and sheer,
Laughter hides, but it's still near.
With glances tossed like silly hats,
I trip on joy, like dancing cats.

A chuckle draped on every frown,
I wear my quirks like a goofy crown.
Each bitter tear, a pickle charm,
Adding flavor, never harm.

To find a smile in sullen days,
I joke around in silly ways.
With starlit whispers from the past,
I learn that joy is meant to last.

In a world where laughs can roam,
I've made a cozy, happy home.
Though shadows linger, never fear,
For every giggle wipes a tear.

Beyond the Horizon of Faded Memories

Beyond the line where laughter dims,
I chase the echoes of silly whims.
Floating on clouds, a feathered tease,
I reminisce with goofy ease.

Forgotten tales of clumsy deeds,
Where every stumble plants new seeds.
Banana peels that make me grin,
Raise spirits higher than they've been.

Through memory's maze, I often trip,
A joyful thought, a playful slip.
Each grin a clue, a wink from fate,
In this wild dance, I oscillate.

With every step, a chuckle stays,
A bright reminder of silly days.
So past the horizon, I will strive,
To find the laughter that keeps me alive.

Traces of Warmth in Cold Memories

I remember the sun, its laugh so bright,
But now it hides, like a cat in fright.
Ice cream cones drip, reminders of cheer,
Yet here I sit, wrapped in winter gear.

Once we danced in puddles, oh what a sight,
Now I trip on snow, not quite as light.
The laughter echoes, a ghostly refrain,
As I question why I jumped on that train.

Memories linger, like crumbs on the floor,
They tickle my toes, then roll out the door.
With mittens in hand, I search for the sun,
But ice skates and flops, well those have their fun!

So here's to the chill, and the warmth that we felt,
To memories made, where laughter has dwelt.
We'll pile on the layers, as winter crops grow,
And toast to the warmth of a thawing snow!

Hues of Nightfall's Secrets

Stars are winking, with mischief anew,
While shadows plot, what mischief to do.
A cat on the prowl, in moonlight she strays,
Chasing her dreams in a dance of delays.

Goblins are giggling in a cackling spree,
While the moon rolls her eyes, 'Oh please, not me!'
The night air is thick with secrets and jest,
As crickets recite their humble request.

The owls are wise, but they're also quite sly,
With each silent swoop, they laugh as they fly.
A jester in darkness, the night plays a game,
While sleepers below, they chase dreams without shame.

Yet morning will stumble, with yawns and a stretch,
Unraveling whispers that night tried to fetch.
In hues of the twilight, we'll tarry and tease,
For every good night, offers giggles and keys!

A Dance in the Wane of Light

As dusk creeps in, it twirls and sways,
We chase after shadows, in a foggy haze.
With flip-flops and fumbles, we stumble right near,
The dance floor is slippery, laughter sincere.

Frogs join the chorus, a croaky delight,
As we trip over roots, wishing for flight.
Glowworms are flashing, a silly parade,
While I wear my best dance moves, all home-made!

Oh, what a scene, with giggles galore,
As the sun takes a bow, behind twilight's door.
The breeze joins the dance, with a tickle and tease,
As we spin in our madness, just doing as we please.

Though the daylight may fade, our spirits ignite,
For we dance in the dark, with stars shining bright.
In the wane of the light, it's all fun and cheer,
As we spin in our laughter, with nothing to fear!

The Afterglow of Celestial Longing

Stars giggle in the dusk,
They tell secrets to the moon.
Crickets play their tiny trumpets,
While fireflies roam like balloons.

A cow jumped over a beam,
Wearing shades and a silly grin.
Dancing like they own the night,
But they're just chasing their own tail spin.

Heaven's foot has left a mark,
In the soft grass where we lay.
With marshmallows flying past,
We chuckle as we drift away.

Oh, the clouds spill laughter too,
Floating high in the sky's embrace.
They trip on each other's fluff,
While we stick our tongues out in grace.

Muffled Heartbeats of Serene Landscapes

Trees whisper to the breeze,
Wearing hats made of leaves.
A squirrel gives a cheesy grin,
While stealing from the thieves.

Frogs croak with careful art,
As if they're crooning a tune.
Their operatic style so grand,
Makes the stars wink at noon.

The river laughs in ripples,
Eddies swirling like a dance.
Fish join in, flopping around,
Their splashes speak of romance.

In the distance, shadows sway,
Playing peek-a-boo with dawn.
Every creature's got a tale,
As they yawn and stretch till gone.

Halos of Light and Fleeting Darkness

A moonbeam pranks the sleepy night,
Tickling crickets in their dreams.
Thoughts of space on pastry plates,
Make unicorns giggle at seams.

Sprinkles of glitter cloud the air,
As comets race in silly lines.
They trip like toddlers on a dare,
Painting laughs on cosmic vines.

Toasters pop with joy at dawn,
Bread dances like it's on a spree.
With jam and laughter all around,
The breakfast table's wild and free.

A shadow squints in the bright sun,
Trying hard to understand.
Life's a jigsaw of pure delight,
In a realm that's awfully grand.

The Latticework of Lost Dreams

Old toys gather dust in closets,
Each one holds a tale to tell.
They plot a raid on sleepy heads,
To break the stillness with a yell.

A kite flutters, a ghostly sight,
Haunting trees with strings so fine.
As children laugh, it dips and dives,
Aerial tricks in a wild design.

Books sigh deeply on their shelves,
Yearning for a quite bustling crowd.
Each page wants to burst with life,
Nudging shelves and feeling proud.

Dreams wrapped tight in laughter's arms,
Revel in their playful schemes.
They dance with us, then slip away,
Like bubbles lost in starry beams.

The Canvas of Vanished Delight

Once painted dreams in hues so bright,
But left to fade in the dimming light.
A masterpiece of mess and cheer,
Did you see that cat? It surely had beer!

Picasso's brush moved with sheer grace,
Yet here I stand, just lost in space.
With splatters of paint on my new shoes,
I laugh, for they were free to choose!

The canvas speaks of days gone by,
Where laughing fairies did fly high.
Yet I tripped over yesterday's bliss,
And laughed so hard I surely missed!

In every stroke, a giggle hides,
For life's a joke where joy abides.
So grab a brush, don't think too long,
Join in this crazy, fun paint song!

Chasing the Flicker of Ethereal Light

Heard whispers from a bulb in flight,
Glimmers darting, oh what a sight!
I ran and tripped on a wayward cat,
He meowed loudly, 'What's wrong with that?'

The glow just danced beyond my reach,
Like a mischief-maker out to teach.
I leaped and leaped, like a fool on fire,
Only to find I lost my desire!

In shadows thick, the light would tease,
Making shadows dance, oh what a breeze!
Just a joke from the universe,
My quest for light turned out quite cursive!

On my quest for brightness, I lost my mind,
The shadows gathered, how unkind!
Yet laughter filled the cracks of night,
For chasing dreams, we hold so tight.

The Flow of Time through Stolen Moments

Time sneaks by like a sneaky thief,
Takes the cookies, leaves me in grief.
I glance away, it's all a blur,
"Hey, where's my cake?" I start to stir.

Moments stolen, sweet and sly,
Tick tock mocks with a gleam in eye.
I blink and stare at my empty plate,
Did time just cheat me—oh, that's just great!

The clocks just giggle, round and round,
As seconds dance, and I can't be found.
But what's to worry, I shrug and grin,
For memories are where the laughs begin!

So here's to time, that playful prank,
For every moment that we tank.
With laughter echoing through the years,
We toast to joy through all the tears!

A Melodic Echo of What Once Was

Tunes of yesteryear weave and sway,
A cacophony of fun and play.
Dancing socks and slippers on feet,
Made our living room feel like a treat!

Oh, that old record, scratchy and clear,
Made us all dance—'twas a jubilant cheer!
Grandma twirled, while Grandpa just swung,
Who knew they had such tasty tongues!

The echoes of laughter fill the room,
Tickling tales of youthful bloom.
Each note carried stories, tales bold,
Of mishaps and giggles, together retold!

As the melody fades into the past,
We hold onto moments that will always last.
So let's dance again on this merry stage,
For laughter's our song at every age!

Chronicles of an Unseen Haven

In a land where daisies daydream,
Socks are lost but never found.
A rabbit dons a hat, it seems,
While turtles race without a sound.

The birds all gossip on the line,
Chirping tales of lost romance.
A frog in boots thinks it's just fine,
To lead the dance, to lead the dance.

Jellybeans rain from the sky,
A cake that giggles as it rolls.
Monkeys wear a tiny tie,
And toast with pickle-flavored shoals.

But in our secret garden stays,
Laughter blooms like flowers bright.
We weave our silly sunlit ways,
While shadows tiptoe out of sight.

A Mosaic of Dreamt Destinies

A pie chart of mismatched socks,
Whimsical in colorful fray.
The clock just laughs, it never clocks,
As dreams jump up to play the day.

Unicorns sip chai with flair,
While penguins join in an old waltz.
Monkeys swing on clouds of air,
And wear mustaches as a pulse.

Cacti sing, but do not dance,
And chairs believe they're superstars.
When jellyfish hold a parade trance,
They'll moonwalk between the cars.

Yet in the kaleidoscope's spins,
Nonsense reigns with joyful cries.
For in our tangled, twisty sins,
We find sunshine in our sighs.

Paintings on the Canvas of Loss

In a world where spoons take flight,
And cats have secret poetry.
The skies are filled with cupcakes bright,
As laughter drips from every tree.

The paintbrush sings a playful tune,
While shadows chase a giggling ghost.
Radio waves dance with the moon,
And toast to all we love the most.

The garden gnomes have tea at three,
Discussing life and grand hotels.
Lemons chatter underneath the tree,
Reminding why we laugh so well.

Yet while the canvas may seem bare,
The colors blend in joyous loss.
Behind each brushstroke, joy we share,
We find the meaning in the toss.

Beneath the Surface of Moonlit Tides

The fish wear hats and dance on waves,
As dolphins twirl in evening's glow.
An octopus plays in the caves,
While seaweed tells the sun below.

Nudibranchs hold a nightly feast,
With pancakes made of ocean's dreams.
A crab recites a poet's least,
While jellyfish bake with moonbeams.

But lurking in the salty air,
Sea turtles spin a tale of lore.
Their laughter splashes everywhere,
As whispers drift upon the shore.

Yet if you dive into the deep,
You'll find a treasure made of fun.
In each wave's cradle, sweet and cheap,
There's joy beneath the setting sun.

The Last Song of the Celestial Isle

On the beach, a crab did dance,
He wore a hat, he took a chance.
Shells applauded, waved with glee,
That funky crustacean, wild and free.

A seagull squawked, it called for snacks,
But all it found were old knick-knacks.
A fish joked, 'You can't be fed,
When all you do is sing instead!'

Palm trees swayed as if to tease,
While coconuts fell with such a breeze.
They rolled along, in playful plight,
Creating chaos, oh what a sight!

At sunset, laughter filled the air,
As friends recounted joys to share.
Each chuckle echoed, bright and bold,
A silly tale, a memory told.

Fragments of the Golden Mirage

A traveler lost, with map askew,
Stumbled upon a town of blue.
Where houses laughed, and windows winked,
He wondered if he really blinked.

An old man danced with gusto grand,
While kids flew kites of cotton candy strands.
They spun and twirled with giddy joy,
Chasing dreams like a little toy.

A merchant sold his wares with sass,
'Get your shoes, they're made of grass!'
They squeaked and squealed, a funny sound,
As giggles spread through all around.

In this land of whims and cheer,
Each moment sparkled, loud and clear.
With every laugh, the sun did rise,
In fragments of joy, the heart complies.

Beneath the Blossoms of Hushed Longing

Under cherry trees, the bees did hum,
A picnic ensued, oh what fun!
Sandwiches stacked like a tower high,
While ants plotted, 'Let's give it a try!'

A dog appeared, his tail a-blur,
He sniffed the crumbs, a gentle purr.
With a leap and a playful roll,
He stole the lunch, oh what a troll!

Friends laughed as they chased their feast,
While blossoms danced, they couldn't cease.
The sky giggled, a ribbon of blue,
A canvas of joy, painted anew.

And in that moment, hearts did soar,
With every bite, we craved for more.
Underneath those petals bright,
We found ourselves in pure delight.

The Gaze Toward Luminous Horizons

At the cliff's edge, a goat stood tall,
He'd tell the world, 'I've seen it all!'
With a smug grin, he surveyed the view,
While tourists snapped photos, one or two.

A parrot squawked, 'What's the fuss?'
'It's just a sunset, come ride the bus!'
Yet every eye was glued in awe,
At colors dripped like a painter's claw.

One person shouted, 'Oh dear me!'
Lost all his snacks, a tragic spree.
But laughter spread, a gentle glow,
As they helped him find what fell below.

With each farewell to golden light,
The stars peeked out, a twinkling sight.
Together they'd laugh until the dawn,
Chasing dreams on this endless lawn.

The Fleeting Mirage of Perfection

Chasing rainbows on a Tuesday,
With ice cream cones in hand.
Laughter spills like melting sugar,
Oh, how sweet the mess we planned.

Wishing well with coins of nonsense,
Dreams float like balloons in air.
Yet the stars seem far from reach,
Find the humor everywhere.

Silly whispers in the evening,
Cats in hats, oh what a sight.
Frogs in tuxedos leap and waltz,
All the wrongs feel so polite.

Hearts that dance like fireflies,
Glow in twilight's soft embrace.
In this chaos of perfection,
Silly smiles claim their own space.

A Symphony of Unseen Wonders

Crickets play the night's concerto,
While the moon forgets its tune.
Yet a squirrel steals the spotlight,
Dancing madly 'neath the moon.

Clouds parade in fluffy lineup,
Impersonating cotton candy.
Laughter echoes, feathery clouds,
Life is just a bit too dandy.

Chasing dreams like lost balloons,
Tangled up in laughter's sway.
Each misplaced note and funny dance,
Turns the night to bright array.

A trumpet blast from kitchen sink,
A rhythm played on pots and pans.
In the symphony of madness,
Every heart joins in the plans.

Caressing the Edges of Tranquility

A cat that thinks it owns the zone,
On the windowsill it sprawls.
Birds debate just what to wear,
While nature laughs and gently calls.

A breeze that tickles all my thoughts,
And nudges daisies to agree.
Sipping tea from wobbly cups,
As laughter bubbles off the tree.

Listened close to whispers soft,
Echoing through the winding lane.
Yet, chaos bubbles hot and quick,
In this calm, we dance again.

Butterflies in polka dots,
Join the fun by twirling near.
Tranquility's a funny place,
Where joy and peace can interfere.

The Abandoned Path to Celestial Realms

A map that leads to nowhere fast,
Marked with laughter, ink of dreams.
Each step taken feels a bit odd,
Yet silly joy is what it seems.

Stars that giggle in the night,
Remind us of a comic plot.
Planets spin in silly ways,
Who knew the cosmos liked to trot?

Abandoned pathways call us back,
To moments lost and tales untold.
We wander in our silly shoes,
Finding treasure in the bold.

So join the dance, let worries fly,
In the void, we laugh and play.
The celestial realms await us all,
In absurdity, we find our way.

Beneath the Boughs of Fragile Whimsy

Beneath the boughs where giggles thrive,
Squirrels debate, inventing a jive.
With nuts as their gems, they frolic around,
In a world of pure jest, joy leaps and bounds.

A rabbit in bowtie hosts tea for the mice,
While the owls keep time with a sprinkle of spice.
Dandelions dance, sharing secrets galore,
In the laughter of leaves, who could ask for more?

Yet a breeze slips by with a mischievous tune,
Knocking hats off the heads as it twirls like a loon.
Grass tickles the feet, all in hearty delight,
Where mirth finds its home, be it day or the night.

Every whispering tree, a storyteller grand,
Revealing the mischief, unplanned and unplanned.
Here, whimsy takes flight on each fluttering leaf,
Reminding us all that joy is belief.

The Enigma of Half-Remembered Joy

In a land where laughter spills like wine,
Buried treasure is candy, quite divine.
A dog in sunglasses chomps on a shoe,
Declaring the world to be one big zoo.

Clouds wear pajamas, oh what a sight!
Pigeons in hats wrangle worms every night.
They argue and squawk, over crumbs and the pie,
In this circus of dreams, we let laughter fly.

Half-remembered joys float on candy clouds,
While moonlight spills secrets to curious crowds.
The sun winks knowingly, as shadows prance,
Inviting the breeze to join in the dance.

Every giggle a riddle, every sigh a clue,
Why the goldfish dons spectacles, who even knew?
Wrap yourself in whimsy, let nonsense breathe,
For joy hides in tales that we sometimes weave.

Veins of Light in Gloom

When darkness grows thick like a stubborn stew,
Fireflies waltz with a glorious view.
They giggle and flicker, their laughter a glow,
In the corners of night, where the whimsy flows.

Mirrors of moonbeams reflect silly dreams,
Cats wear bowties and play in sunbeams.
A jester of dusk juggles stars in the air,
While crickets recite their most fabulous fare.

Gloom hums a tune, a rather odd song,
In the shadows, a parade of absurdities throng.
The glow from the moon, an uncertain delight,
Paints portraits of giggles that flash in the night.

And when morning sneaks in with a wink and a smile,
The folks of the night dance just one more mile.
In veins of sweet laughter and zest so profound,
The world is a canvas where whimsy is found.

Where Shadows Dance with Radiance

In corners where sunlight can't seem to creep,
Shadows tell stories, secrets to keep.
A chair with no legs plays hopscotch with spades,
As whispers of whimsy become grand parades.

Lampshades are laughing, what a silly sight,
Chasing dust bunnies that bounce with delight.
The floorboards join in, they creak with a shake,
As shadows pirouette for their own lovely sake.

Mirrored reflections toss giggles around,
As light takes a bow, then leaps from the ground.
The clocks all tick-tock in rhythm and rhyme,
Making mischief in time: oh, isn't it prime?

So join in the dance, where the shadows sway,
With each little flicker, let laughter have play.
In this bright interlude, we indulge our delight,
Where shadows dance boldly, embracing the light.

Restoration of the Sweetest Illusions

In the depths of my warmest dreams,
I find the spoons with silver beams.
They stir my soup in curious ways,
and dance around in dapper plays.

Yet beware the chef with flashy hats,
he steals the laughs like sneaky cats.
While gumdrops melt in bright sunlight,
the menu reads, 'It's quite a sight!'

A pie of clouds floats up on high,
with giggles brewed from a lemon pie.
Oh, what fun in this wild delight,
when jellybeans pop and take flight!

So here's to dreams, both sweet and bright,
where tiny giraffes dance in moonlight.
With silly hats and polka dots,
restoring joy to forget-me-nots.

Dreams Woven in Iris and Gold

Iris blooms sing tales untold,
atop a hill with threads of gold.
With rainbows spun on silly shoes,
yesterday's shades reveal the blues.

In fields of whimsy, socks do chase,
while butterflies have paper grace.
They swirl around like frisky bees,
while ticklish grass hums gentle tease.

A turtle whispers to a frog,
who jumps so high, he lands in fog.
With laughter echoing like a bell,
they plot a scheme to break the spell.

And here we weave our dreams divine,
with jigsaw pieces made of twine.
The colors blend in hues of cheer,
and giggles grow when friends are near.

Ciphers in the Garden of Wishes

Beneath a bush with lollipop blooms,
a cat in shoes dispels the glooms.
With riddles tied to carrot strings,
a symphony of joy it brings.

The gnome spins tales of cookie thieves,
who laugh and dance among the leaves.
While sparrows sing top-secret songs,
where garden gnomes grow mighty bongs.

A patch of grass that giggles bright,
binds secrets with a sparkly kite.
In sneaky rhymes, we hide our hopes,
a maze of carrots, ginger ropes.

So come and play where shadows sway,
where all our silly dreams can stay.
In whispers soft, the garden swishes,
and giggles bloom with secret wishes.

Beneath the Glistening Facade

Underneath a glimpse of cheer,
a squirrel holds a pint of beer.
His buddies laugh, a funny sight,
as moonbeams spark in the cool night.

A circus tent of candy stripes,
where ants ride bikes and play inipes.
They juggle crumbs and sip on juice,
and maybe dance the funky moose!

With shadows cast from neon dreams,
a lizard prances on sunshine beams.
He tells of tales from days of old,
wrapped snug in stories sweet and bold.

So lift your glass to silly fun,
where joy and laughter always run.
And though the world may spin and twirl,
we find our bliss in this crazy whirl.

Mysteries of the Lamp-lit Garden

In the garden where night lights play,
Dancing shadows lead us astray.
Bees in tuxedos sipping on tea,
Whispering secrets, just you and me.

Gnomes gossip 'neath the moon's silly grin,
Debating if fortune could ever begin.
A cat in a top hat, what a surprise,
Laughs at the flowers with bemused eyes.

Fireflies join in a conga line,
While we ponder the taste of good wine.
Camping here, could we dare to sleep?
Or do the daisies want company to keep?

So let's linger a while longer, dear,
Amongst the leaves where the laughter's clear.
For every twinkle in star's parade,
Hides a joke that the crickets have made.

Illusions within the Embrace of Silence

Inside whispers echo, absurd and loud,
As mushrooms wearing glasses gather a crowd.
A snail with a monocle ponders the fuss,
While silence giggles; it's quite the plus.

The wind chuckles, playing peek-a-boo,
With shadows pretending they're something new.
A frog breaks the silence with a loud croak,
Declaring his reign as the garden's folk.

Twirling in circles, the plants sway and bend,
To hear the secrets that night may send.
Laughter spills out from the lilacs tonight,
Painting the dark in colors so bright.

So let's tiptoe on laughter, hand in hand,
Under stars where gags never get bland.
For in the folds of this silence we find,
The cosmic humor that tickles the mind.

Shimmering Waves of Dusk's Desires

As the sun winks, the waves start to glow,
A dance of fish in a limbo, oh so slow.
Seagulls wear sunglasses, posing for fame,
As they dive and sway in this game of the same.

Mysterious mermaids swim with a laugh,
Debating if dolphins should take a bath.
Shells play charades, as tides pull away,
Crafting stories of whims, day after day.

Crabs breakdance on sand, what a sight,
While surfboards gossip about the last flight.
Every wave carries a comedic tale,
Of how many fish lost their heads to a nail.

In the twilight, where dreams come alive,
Frogs in the ocean begin to dive.
So let's surf through the laughter, my friend,
And ride this wave of fun till the end.

Constellations on the Edge of Regret

Stars tumble down to give us a wink,
As they gossip about what we think.
A comet can't help but roll on the floor,
Laughing at planets and what they adore.

Shooting stars race with dreams gone wrong,
Trying to write a very short song.
But all that comes out is a silly tune,
That makes the night giggle under the moon.

The Milky Way spills its secrets out loud,
While satellites chuckle at the silly crowd.
Asteroids dance in a clumsy ballet,
Tripping on stardust, they sway and they splay.

So here we ponder under this vast dome,
With laughter wrapped up in celestial foam.
For every regret is a star that's bright,
Shining a little more to spark some delight.

Secrets Beneath the Canopy

Under leaves, a squirrel schemes,
Hiding nuts in secret dreams.
Why do they giggle? It's quite absurd,
For a nutty secret is no real word!

Mushrooms dance at midnight glee,
Pretending they're a wild ballet.
Fungi dressed in nature's rags,
Prancing proudly, oh the jags!

The wise old owl, a judge, a bard,
Sipping tea, calling it 'retard'.
Horace the hedgehog writes his sonnet,
But only those bugs hear his sonnet!

So keep your secrets, sly and sly,
In the leafy shade where the giggles lie.
For the real treasure isn't in the chest,
But in the laughter, that's truly the best!

Visions of a Celestial Mirage

Stars fell down like confetti grace,
As goats in cloaks take to space.
Uranus grumbles, 'this isn't fair,'
While Martians dance in underwear!

The moonlight turns to pudding thick,
And starlight tickles, a cosmic trick.
Neptune swaggers, 'I'm the coolest one',
While solar flares in laughter run!

Space crabs dance with three left feet,
On Saturn's rings, they just can't beat.
Galactic chaos in celestial bins,
Asteroids giggle, saying, 'Let's spin!'

Floating dreams in milky skies,
Where laughter drips like moonlit pies.
In this vastness, we're all absurd,
As stars in tutus weave the unheard!

The Twilight of Lost Bliss

Sunset's blush, the world's a clown,
Twilight antics with chipmunk frown.
A rainbow slides on banana peels,
Oh, the giggles, what it reveals!

Fireflies do the jig at dusk,
While crickets chat of wheat and musk.
They wear tiny hats, too fancy to share,
In the twilight realm, life's a fair!

The moon yawns wide, bears a big grin,
Telling shadows it's time to spin.
A raccoon steals cookies, oh what a sight,
In this sneaky game under the night!

So raise your voice, sing loud, not meek,
For lost bliss isn't ever bleak.
It's laughter echoing in the mist,
As twilight giggles, you can't resist!

Crumbling Castles in the Sky

Floating towers of candy and fluff,
With lollipop knights, oh, isn't that tough?
But watch them tumble, giggling in flight,
As gummy bears laugh at the silly sight!

Clouds wear crowns, a fluffy brigade,
Building castles in plans that won't fade.
Yet rainstorms bring their grand collapse,
And the kingdom erupts in giggly mishaps!

The sun peeks out, says, 'What a mess!',
While wind-whirl dancers stutter in dress.
Do castles crumble? Oh yes, indeed!
But laughter reigns in our heart's great need!

So let the skies fall, let the laughter soar,
In crumbling dreams, we can't ignore.
For in the splinters of our grand schemes,
We find our joy in the silliest dreams!

Whispers of Forgotten Eden

In a tree where woes take flight,
A squirrel boasts of nuts at night.
He claims he's king of all he sees,
While birds just laugh and tease him, please.

A blossom blooms, then trips a bee,
"Watch your step!" it buzzes free.
The fruits hang low, with faces bright,
But none can pick them without a fight.

As whispers float through leaves and vines,
A rabbit writes his quirky lines.
He jots down tales of veggie dreams,
While puddles chuckle in warm beams.

So join this feast of silly glee,
Where laughter grows on every tree.
In Eden's echoes, let us play,
And chase the mundane away today.

Beneath the Veil of Serenity

Where daisies chat in gentle rows,
A turtle struts in mismatched clothes.
He tells the daisies, "I'm so fast!"
But trips and falls, his tale surpass-ed.

An owl debates with a cheeky crow,
"I'm wise!" said he, with status quo.
But all the critters roll their eyes,
As he forgets what's in disguise.

A butterfly spins tales so grand,
But flaps away before it's planned.
"I'll bring you gems!" it flutters loud,
Yet finds just dust, and wine in cloud.

So here beneath this calm facade,
A wacky world is just as odd.
With laughter stitched through every seam,
In peace, we dance and wildly dream.

Echoes of a Dreamed Utopia

In fields where dreams are chased in flight,
A goat thinks he can sway the night.
He boasts of stars he plans to eat,
While dancing sheep just laugh in heat.

A jester frog, with hat so bright,
Leaps on lilies, what a sight!
He croaks a tune that's off-key strung,
Yet every bug still hums along.

As sunlight paints the day in gold,
A hedgehog's secrets come unfold.
He says he hides the juiciest tales,
While otters giggle in the gales.

Through echoes of this dreamy land,
We wander with our hearts so grand.
With chuckles bright and smiles in store,
Each moment here means so much more.

The Lament of Hidden Gardens

A garden blooms where no one goes,
Yet gnomes complain of grass that grows.
They argue who has lost a hat,
While ants march by, all squeaky chat.

The roses cry of lack of sun,
While daisies shout, "Let's have some fun!"
With petals folded, they enlist,
For wild events that can't be missed.

While shadows play tag with the light,
A bunny hops, seeking delight.
It trips and rolls, a comical scene,
And giggles echo, such a routine.

So in this nook, with funny strife,
Resides the quirkiest garden life.
Where laughter grows from every crack,
And whispers dwell, never hold back.

Reflections in the Pool of Longing

A frog in a tux, quite dapper indeed,
Hops at the edge, where dreams take their lead.
He whispers to lilies, with gossip so sweet,
"Haven't you heard? Love's hard to defeat!"

Clouds overhead chuckle, they dance to the breeze,
While the frog, lost in thought, leans back with such ease.

Ripples of longing, a splash of desire,
He dreams of a princess; his heart's on fire!

But the pond's just a puddle, his hopes float in vain,
A tale of misfortune, wrapped up in the rain.
With a leap and a croak, he resigns to the night,
"Tomorrow, dear me, I'll get it just right!"

The Conundrum of Chasing Light

There once was a moth who loved neon glow,
He fancied himself quite the star of the show.
But each time he fluttered, he met with a zap,
"Chasing is fun, but this really feels crap!"

His friends all just laughed, "It's a light, dear friend!
You must learn the lesson that all must attend!"
Yet he flew on, questing, headstrong and bold,
Ignoring the wisdom, for sparkles and gold!

He twirled and he swayed, like a dancer in flight,
Until one fateful night, he flew far too bright.
With a singe and a scream, he dodged out of sight,
"I guess I'll just stick to the moonlight tonight!"

Shadows Beneath the Lovers' Arches

Beneath the grand arches, two lovers did sway,
They whispered sweet nothings, ignoring the day.
But shadows, mischievous, crept close with delight,
And chuckled aloud at their whimsical plight!

"Oh dear, can you get any closer?" they teased,
While the lovers just giggled, delightfully pleased.
"We're the stars of this show, so dim down your glee!"
But shadows just danced and said, "Wait and see!"

A sneeze from the left, a tumble from right,
And suddenly, love turned into a fright.
With laughter they stumbled and fell through the grass,
The shadows, still chuckling, just twirled and passed!

The Mirage of Enchanted Hills

In a land where the hills glimmered bright with deceit,
Lived a goat with a dream of gourmet fine meat.
He climbed every peak, his ambition so grand,
Only to find it was all just a scam!

Illusions of apples adorned every tree,
While the goat munched on rocks, resenting his spree.
"Oh where is my banquet, my feast fit for kings?"
As the wind played its tune, and the valley just sings!

He bumped into rabbits, who laughed at his plight,
"Dude, it's just a mirage, don't go chasing the light!"
But the goat, ever hopeful, just grinned with a cheer,
"Next time I'll just dine with my friends over here!"

Lighthouses in the Mist of Regret

A lighthouse stands with a wink and a wave,
Its light blinks out like a funny old rave.
Seagulls squawk jokes to the waves down below,
While the fish swim by, just putting on a show.

The fog rolls in like a bad stand-up bit,
And boats drift by, stuck in the skit.
A captain shouts, 'Where's the treasure, my friend?'
But the only gold is the sunshine to lend.

The tide pulls back, does a little dance,
As sailors all laugh, given half a chance.
Regret's just a pun, with a twist of the sea,
A lighthouse laughs on, full of glee.

So here's to the beacon, with humor in light,
Navigating through gloom, with laughter in sight.
For every regret, there's a chuckle to find,
A lighthouse in fog, exuding bright mind.

A Tapestry Woven with Unfulfilled Yearnings

Oh, what a quilt of dreams hung on a line,
Stitched with the hopes of a world so divine!
There's a pocket for wishes, all crumpled and wrinkled,
Each thread tells a joke that left the crowd crinkled.

Threads of ambition interlace with despair,
How did I end up in this old plush chair?
With patterns of longing and colors so bold,
Each twinkle of yarn has a funny tale told.

Under the fabric, dreams often play,
They giggle and tumble; they're wacky and gay.
The weaver, bemused, checks the knots that she made,
While squirrels drop walnuts in her grand parade.

So raise up your glasses to this quirk of a piece,
Each yearning a laugh that never found peace.
A tapestry woven with threads that collide,
Where humor and sorrow so splendidly hide.

Straying Among the Fragments of Hope

Lost in a maze of my scattered dreams,
I stumble on hopes like a clown with no schemes.
Each fragment a chuckle, a giggle, a blip,
As I trip on a thought—oh, there go my lips!

Hope's just a jigsaw of pieces awry,
Puzzles in corners where misfits all lie.
I laugh at the edges, all jagged and wild,
A mosaic of folly, enchanting and mild.

Among the mischief, a spark lighted bright,
With every wrong turn, I've found sheer delight.
Straying through shards, I trip again and again,
Laughter's the glue, turning losses to gains.

So here's to the fragments, all whimsical cheer,
For in every mishap, there's something to hear.
Amidst the confusion, I dance with my fate,
Straying with glee, isn't life just great?

Subtle Hues of Forgotten Splendor

From a palette of pasts that whisper and sigh,
I paint with the brush of a well-cooked pie.
Each color a giggle, round the edges they blur,
As sunsets remind me of pickle-flavored fur.

The hues mix and mingle, creating a mess,
A canvas of laughter, what more could I guess?
Forgotten are sorrows, wrapped in silly hues,
I chuckle, and wonder if blueberries snooze.

Each stroke tells a tale, with a wink and a nudge,
Of autumn's bright belly and winter's sweet fudge.
Splendor that flickers in palm-sized delight,
As I sip on my eggnog, all fuzzy and bright.

So let's cheer for the colors, the laughter they bring,
For in every smudge, there's a reason to sing.
Subtle hues paint the moments we trace,
In the laughter of life, we all find our place.

Lurking Beneath the Olive Tree

Beneath the olives, whispers float,
A squirrel's dance in a tiny coat.
He plots and schemes with great delight,
To swipe my lunch without a fight.

The sunbeam's laughter, soft and bright,
As fruit flies plot their daring flight.
I toss a crumb, while giggles swell,
'Best serve it fresh, or time will tell!'

With every bite, the tales unwind,
Of bees who buzz with secrets kind.
In this green den where mischief grows,
A comedy that only nature knows.

Leaves whisper tunes of forgotten lore,
As I chase after crumbs on the floor.
The squirrel grins, it's all a game,
In this olive nook, we're all the same.

Unraveled Threads of Elysium

In fields of thought, where dreams take flight,
I tripped on clouds of sheer delight.
A goat appeared with a knowing nod,
As I fell flat in a pose quite odd.

Threads of yarn spun tales so bright,
I tangled my heart, oh what a sight!
With every stitch, a giggle grew,
As cats danced in colors brand new.

Together we laughed at the cosmic dance,
In the wooly worlds, we took our chance.
A stitch of laughter, a tangle of cheer,
In this wobbly weave, there's nothing to fear.

So here we wander, with yarn in tow,
Crafting mishaps where wild ideas flow.
In this makeshift haven, we're all quite free,
Dancing around in our tapestry.

The Silent Allure of Hidden Realms

Within the bushes, secrets lie,
A hedgehog sighs as I walk by.
He raises a brow with a knowing gleam,
'What's that, my friend? A wild snack dream?'

Frogs throw parties with a croaky cheer,
As fireflies twinkle, drawing near.
I join their dance with two left feet,
A clumsy jester, can't take a seat!

With every hop, the moonlight beams,
And fills the night with giggly dreams.
Wishing on stars, we bow in glee,
In a world where laughter sets us free.

So let us wander in realms uncharted,
Where nonsense thrives, and joy is started.
With whispers of magic, we'll all belong,
In these hidden realms where we sing our song.

Cradled Beneath the Starlit Veil

Under the stars, I lay with glee,
Imagining shapes like a laughing bee.
'Is that a horse, or did I snore?'
A cosmic giggle from the great outdoors.

Each twinkle mocks my half-asleep muse,
As foxes gossip about my snooze.
They wiggle their tails, a sight so right,
Chasing the moon till the end of night.

The comets zoom past with a cheeky wink,
While I ponder on life's great pink drink.
Rumors spread fast, laughter's the key,
In dreams, we're all wild and utterly free.

So with every star, my heart will sail,
In the tales spun beneath this starlit veil.
Let laughter echo, let merriment sing,
In this cozy cosmos, forever we spring.

Veins of Gold in the Ruins of Sorrow

Amidst the rubble, dreams collide,
Bouncing off walls where smiles reside.
Golden laughter in cracked mirrors,
Sipping sunlight, ignoring the terrors.

Jesters dance on the hollowed ground,
Where hope and humor can still be found.
A treasure map drawn with coffee stains,
Leading to joy through laughter's chains.

In the attic, a dust bunny reigns,
Counting secrets, ignoring the pains.
With each tick of the clock's weird song,
We laugh at what we've done wrong.

Finding gems in the cluttered mess,
Gilded moments, who could guess?
In the ruins, we toss our cares,
Trading woes for giggles and glares.

Pursuing Shadows in a Lost Paradise

Chasing silhouettes on a foggy night,
Tripping on laughter, oh what a fright!
Every shadow's a whiff of fun,
Laughing at ghosts who can't outrun.

Wandering paths that lead to surprise,
Unexpected dance with butterflies.
In this realm where light bends and twirls,
Even the flowers wear silly pearls.

A feast of giggles under starry skies,
Whimsy blooms where the oddity lies.
Piecing together a puzzle that's cracked,
In the chaos, the joy is intact.

So grab a friend and skip down the lane,
Whistling loudly, driving folks insane.
In this madcap chase, forget the strife,
Finding delight in the quirks of life.

The Silent Song of Forgotten Fables

Once upon a time in a land so quirky,
Fables whispered, but not so perky.
The heroes stumbled, the villains tripped,
    Every grand tale a comic script.

Dragons puffed smoke, but forgot their flame,
Napping through battles, what a shame!
Knights would joust on pogo sticks,
    As laughter echoed in the mix.

Witches tried spells that went awry,
Turning toads into pies, oh my!
In the quiet of this whimsical lore,
Every old tale cracked up the floor.

So let your heart wander where nonsense roams,
In forgotten fables, laughter finds homes.
With every misstep, with every blunder,
The silent song brings joyful wonder.

Echoes of a Distant Reverie

Whispering dreams in a twilight haze,
Echoes bounce in silly ways.
Imagination spins a wild tale,
With rubber chickens setting sail.

In a meadow of mismatched socks,
Time plays tricks, it laughs and mocks.
Pillows float like clouds in the sky,
Bouncing ideas that soar up high.

A laugh in the distance, a playful shout,
The serious things just fade out.
In reveries where the absurd sings,
Every mishap brings funny flings.

So dance along this whimsical ride,
Join the parade with arms open wide.
In echoes of joy, let your spirit soar,
In a world of laughter, who needs more?

The Paradox of Perfect Haven

In the land of endless smiles,
Where the sun drinks fizzy pop,
Laughter floats on cotton clouds,
And all the giggles never stop.

Yet beneath the shiny surface,
A squirrel's plotting some grand theft,
He steals the peach of joy we think,
Now there's sticky chaos left!

The birds sing tunes so upbeat,
But watch that frog dance by the tree,
With his croak-turned-rap career,
He's the buzz in this jubilee!

Beneath the merry, quirky sky,
Lies a banana peel or two,
One slip and giggles turn to screams,
In this haven, who knew?

Ghosts of a Radiant Past

In this whimsically lost realm,
Ghosts of giggles float around,
They wear mismatched polka dots,
And sing off-key, but oh-so-proud.

Once upon a time, they pranced,
Like daisies in a fever dream,
Now they trip on cobblestones,
Spilling custard in a stream.

With faded tales of vibrant hues,
They tell of ice cream that won't melt,
But bite a cone, and it's a trick!
Sudden drips are cleverly dealt.

These joyful phantoms dance around,
In a carnival of silly glee,
Haunting this kooky wonderland,
Where laughter's free, as it should be!

The Flicker of Wandering Light

There's a light that winks at me,
As I skip through fields of fluff,
It dances like it's lost for sure,
But hey, is being lost that tough?

It leads me to a donut shop,
Where frosting clouds float in the air,
But even there, that light just beams,
And ignites a game of 'Who Dares?'

Chasing beams like mischievous sprites,
Through puddles that giggle and splash,
Only to find at bitter end,
I narrowly escaped a crash!

Yet in this gleeful chaos,
A silver lining takes its place,
For laughter always flickers bright,
In this curious cosmic race.

Ephemeral Grace in a Stolen Moment

A moment sighs between the cracks,
Where time and giggles intertwine,
I grab a slice of joy so sweet,
Before it runs away, divine.

Caught in a dance with my bad hair,
Twists and turns, a puzzling show,
My socks are mismatched 'gasp!' we say,
Who knew fashion's such a blow?

But here, in stolen bits of fun,
Laughter bubbles up like soda,
Jumping on chairs like rambunctious fleas,
In a world that's turned loco!

Ephemerally danced away,
But moments linger on the vine,
So let's embrace this silly grace,
With a wink and a slice of time!

www.ingramcontent.com/pod-product-compliance
Lightning Source LLC
Chambersburg PA
CBHW072132070526
44585CB00016B/1643